Original title:
Tales of the Fiddle-Leaf

Copyright © 2025 Creative Arts Management OÜ
All rights reserved.

Author: Levi Montgomery
ISBN HARDBACK: 978-1-80581-882-3
ISBN PAPERBACK: 978-1-80581-409-2
ISBN EBOOK: 978-1-80581-882-3

Beneath the Veil of Verdance

In a room full of leaves so bright,
A plant wore a hat, much to my delight.
It swayed to the sound of a breeze so bold,
While my cat eyed the foliage, daring and cold.

With shoes on its roots, it danced all around,
Making me laugh, what a sight I had found!
I joined in the jig, twirling with glee,
Yet tripped on the mat, oh dear, not the tree!

A Symphony of Roots

A root conductor waved with flair,
While the leaves sang songs from a highchair.
Each branch was a solo, oh what a surprise,
Even the dust bunnies danced in disguise.

The water droplets fell like a cheerful rain,
As my fiddle-leaf friend just snickered in vain.
It tickled the soil where the earthworms reside,
And I laughed so hard, I nearly cried!

Lanterns in the Indoor Jungle

Beneath a canopy of bright green charms,
My plants throw parties with their leafy arms.
They sip on sunshine, like it's a fine brew,
While I watch in wonder, what else can they do?

A spider dropped by, dressed up for the show,
Spinning wild webs, put on quite a glow.
With a wink and a twist, it stole the spotlight,
And left me chuckling, feeling just right.

Dreams Among the Evergreen

In a jungle of pots with a view so sweet,
A bonsai is gossiping, oh what a feat!
It spilled all the beans on the plant next door,
Who thought it could sing, oh what a bore!

We chuckled aloud, the air full of cheer,
As a sloth made his way, moving quite clear.
It took him an hour just to cross the floor,
But when he got there, we all wanted more!

Elegy for an Urban Oasis

In a pot so snug and tight,
Leaves dance under urban light.
A squirrel sneaks, a cat on prowl,
I laugh as they stage a growl.

The rain taps on the window glass,
While I sip tea, oh how it shines!
Amid concrete, green dreams amass,
The city's pulse with fate entwines.

Oh green gal in the lively room,
You whisper secrets to the dawn.
With every leaf, I chase the gloom,
As joy unfolds, my worries yawn.

So here's to you, my leafy mate,
In laughter, we shall simply thrive.
When chaos reigns, just hold your fate,
And we'll keep dancing, oh so live!

Resilience in Potbound Soil

Stuck in a pot, but cheer we keep,
Roots juggle dreams, in dirt they leap.
The sun's a tease, it tickles high,
We laugh as clouds parade on by.

Oh stubborn sprout with hopes so bold,
You try to stretch, yet fate's on hold.
Chasing rays with all your might,
But here we stand, a leafy sight.

A gust of wind within the maze,
You sway and twist in leafy praise.
With neighbors close, we steal the scene,
In our small world, we reign supreme.

Though potbound, never will we pout,
We offer laughter, that's our route.
In urban tales of soil and sun,
We bloom in jest, and call it fun!

Reflections of a Sunlit Room

In sunlight's glow, the shadows play,
Each leaf a story on display.
With every beam, they twirl and prance,
We chuckle at this leafy dance.

The window frames a leafy muse,
While laughter drips like morning dew.
A burst of green, a hint of gold,
These quiet tales of joy unfold.

Dust dances, motes in flight,
With joyous whispers, hearts ignite.
In every corner, life is bold,
Turning laughs into tales retold.

So here I sit, with muted cheer,
In sunlit rooms, we persevere.
With green companions by my side,
In laughter's light, we'll always bide!

Gardener's Quiet Confessions

In my garden with soil so rich,
I laugh at weeds that like to hitch.
With watering can, I hum a tune,
To playful roots that twist and swoon.

Each sprout holds secrets, leafy jest,
As I confess, they're truly blessed.
I water love, but sometimes dread,
When pests arrive, I flip my head.

Oh dear companions, green and bright,
You crack me up with every sight.
In daily battles, side by side,
We share our laughs, with hope as guide.

So let my thoughts in quiet roll,
As laughter fills this vibrant bowl.
Among petals, I find my peace,
In plants, the joy will never cease!

The Seasons of a Leafy Life

In spring, they sprout, so bold and bright,
Dancing in the sunlight, oh what a sight!
A leaf in summer, lounging with ease,
Whispering secrets to the buzzing bees.

Autumn's laughter turns them gold,
They giggle as they break from the mold.
Winter, cold, they play hide and seek,
Wrapping in blankets, it's cozy and weak.

Vignettes of Homegrown Beauty

In a pot on the sill, lives a cheeky sprout,
With dreams of the garden, it gives a shout.
"Hey! Look at me, growing up tall!"
Knocking on windows, having a ball!

With freckles of dirt on its cheerful face,
It poses for photos, what a fun place!
Sipping on sunshine, it blushes in green,
Homegrown beauty, always a scene.

The Language of Chlorophyll

A conversation with leaves, oh what a fun chat,
They gossip and giggle, imagine that!
"In sunlight we bask, in shadows we play,
Making a dance for the bright sunny day!"

Chlorophyll's whispers, a vibrant delight,
Tickling the air, a jubilant flight.
"Let's paint us a rainbow, from green to gold!"
They chuckle together, as stories unfold.

Shadows Cast by Living Green

Casting shadows that prance on the floor,
Each leaf tells a story, inviting for more.
They stretch in the late sun, playing a game,
Whispering nonsense, oh what a shame!

Twirling and swirling in breezy delight,
Their laughter echoes, a whimsical sight.
Beneath the canopy, a silly charade,
Where shadows and leaves form a playful parade.

Harmonies in a Sunlit Room

In a corner sat a plant, so spry,
With leaves that waved as days drifted by.
It giggled at the sun that beamed,
And whispered secrets while others dreamed.

A slight breeze came, a tickle, a tease,
The leaves shook head, 'We're not here to freeze!'
A spider spun tales in a web so fine,
While the plant just swayed, sipping on sunshine.

Echoes in the Canopy

Beneath the greens of a mighty tree,
A little leaf laughed, 'Oh, isn't it free?'
It teased the ants marching along,
'You can't catch me, I'm too spry and strong!'

With a flutter and a dance, it stole the show,
As squirrels below murmured, 'Look at that glow!'
Each sway and twist was a joyous feat,
A leafy diva with nimble feet.

Chronicles of a Lonely Stem

Once was a stem, standing up tall,
Wishing for friends to dance in the hall.
It stretched and it sighed, 'Where can they be?'
Then tickled by laughter, it giggled with glee.

A curious bud peeked out from the side,
Joined in the fun, no more lonely pride.
They jived and they twirled, a leafy ballet,
A friendship was formed in a silly display.

The Dance of Quivering Fronds

In a pot by the window, two fronds came to play,
They wiggled and jiggled throughout the day.
'Let's dance beneath air, and jump to the tune!'
They swayed to the whispers of summer's bright moon.

Brought forth by the wind, they twirled with delight,
Chasing the shadows as day turned to night.
With laughter so bright, they mocked all the gloom,
Spreading their joy around in the room.

The Dialogue of Leaves

In the pot where sunlight beams,
A leaf turns, spilling its dreams.
"I'm the star of this small stage,"
Said the sprout with a leafy gaze.

"You think you're all that and more?"
Said the next with a little score.
"You just wiggle in the breeze,"
While I sway with the greatest ease.

"With every wind, I toss and play,"
"Oh please, save your jokes for the day!"
Roots whisper jokes deep below,
In this plant comedy show.

Laughter sprouts in every vein,
Underneath the gentle rain.
With humor weaving through their life,
Indoor tales without the strife.

Echoes of Nature Indoors

In the corner where shadows fall,
Green giants gather, standing tall.
"What's your secret?" asks the vine,
"to look so lush, to twist and twine."

"I just drink from the morning light,"
Said the fern with leaves oh-so-bright.
"And throw in a sprinkle of fun,"
"That's how I grow, just like the sun!"

A cactus chimes in with a grin,
"I prefer a dry but witty spin!"
"You're all softies, but it's okay,"
"Let's throw a sass party today!"

Branches sway with a hint of glee,
Echoing laughter, wild and free.
In this room where plants reside,
Nature's jokes cannot be denied.

Serene Growth in Urban Corners

Amidst the concrete jungle's roar,
Potted greens burst through the floor.
"Can you hear the city's hum?"
Whispered one leaf, just being fun.

"I thrive on noise and thick, thick air,"
Chimed the cactus with a flair.
"While others flee to quiet streets,"
"I just groove to the urban beats!"

"Are you crazy?" teased the tree,
"I'd like some peace, and maybe tea!"
"But where's the thrill in silent life?"
"It's the city buzz I want to rife!"

United in their leafy quips,
On windy days, they'd shake their hips.
In urban corners, plants all know,
Life's a comedy, row by row.

Chronicles from the Soil

Down below, where whispers dwell,
Worms recount their greatest tales.
"Just yesterday, I found a shoe!"
Laughed the worm, amidst the goo.

"I found a slice of pizza crust,"
Said a bug, with the utmost trust.
"Not a crumb, but a whole square,"
"What a feast, beyond compare!"

Roots debate their tangled fate,
"This soil's prime, we are first-rate!"
"But watch your growth; don't peek above,"
"Or else you'll lose what soil you love!"

In dark earth, where secrets lie,
Life unfolds, oh me, oh my!
Chronicles spun from earthy cheer,
Nature's humor, loud and clear.

Whispers of Growth and Grace

Leaves chatter softly in their swing,
They giggle as they drink in spring.
With stems that dance in joyful sway,
Who knew plants had so much to say?

A pot of soil, a hearty splash,
They gossip about the neighbor's stash.
A sprinkle here, a little there,
Oh, the laughter that fills the air!

Sunbeams tickle, shadows prance,
Every inch a leafy dance.
Roots tickling under the ground,
In whispered secrets, joy is found.

Bugs sneaking in for a free snack,
With a wiggle, those greens fight back.
In a world where silence is rare,
Fiddles find fun everywhere!

The Legacy of Forgotten Gardens

In corners once lush, now overgrown,
Whispers of laughter echo, alone.
Plants that once held splendor bright,
Share tales of mischief in the night.

Broken pots, yet they still jest,
Competing for who's the very best.
Vines embrace, then pull apart,
A tangle of joy, a work of art.

Garden gnomes with crooked grins,
Roll their eyes at the world's spins.
In shadows, their secrets bubble high,
An audience of worms, watching nigh.

Once a patch of pride and grace,
Now a haven for wild embrace.
Among the weeds, they raise a cheer,
In the orchestra of forgotten years!

Echoes of Life in a Sunlit Space

Morning beams tickle leaves awake,
Stretching wide, a green earthquake.
Mossy whispers drift through the air,
As sunlight dances without a care.

A ladybug laughs, plump on a stem,
Declaring this spot her precious gem.
Caught in a weave of joy and light,
Every moment is pure delight.

Buzzy bees in a flower trance,
Stumbling over their floral dance.
Frolicking blooms spread wide their arms,
Chasing giggles with sunny charms.

In every crack, a story's spun,
Life weaves a path for silly fun.
With every rustle, voices blend,
In this gathering, hearts transcend.

Nurtured Dreams of Silence and Green

Quiet thoughts grow deep like roots,
In the stillness, creativity shoots.
A tiny sprout with a cheeky grin,
I wonder just where all this begins.

Dreams whisper secrets to the ground,
Wiggly worms hum a silly sound.
Nature's playground, a world of play,
In every leaf, a dance of sway.

Nighttime brings the stars to cheer,
While crickets giggle, 'we have no fear!'
Under the moon, the plants all talk,
In shadows thick, they have a walk.

Every bud tells a funny tale,
Of recent rains and the sun's hail.
In harmony, they thrive and preen,
In this lush wild, all's quite serene.

The Solitary Leaf's Journey

A leaf set out on a grand quest,
To find a friend, it thought for the best.
It rolled and it tumbled, oh what a sight,
In search of a buddy to share the delight.

It danced with the dust, performed with a grin,
Hoping to find someone to spin.
But all it found were old soda cans,
And bees who were busy, with honey in plans.

With a flutter and flap, it waved at the sun,
"Join me in silliness, let's have some fun!"
But the sun just chuckled, shining so bright,
While the leaf laughed back, what a glorious sight!

Then off to the park, it swirled and it swayed,
Dreaming of friendships, while never dismayed.
Though alone on the journey, it surely would find,
That laughter's the key to a flourishing mind.

Embracing Nature's Embrace

In the garden, a sprout had a laugh,
It giggled at bugs, what a comical staff!
With ants on parade, and a worm doing splits,
Nature's own circus, with quirky little bits.

A flower said, "Hey! Want to twirl with me?"
The sprout gave a nod, oh what glee!
Together they chuckled, around and around,
In the arms of the earth, joy truly was found.

The sun peeked in, with a wink and a grin,
"Do you two need a hand? Let's make this a win!"
They all took a bow, what a splendid display,
As butterflies joined in, swaying ballet.

In the heart of the garden, laughter rang true,
With every bright bloom, a sparkly view.
When nature's your friend, the supply never ends,
With a giggle and a dance, all the world bends.

Portrait of a Potted Dream

In a pot by the window, a dream took a stand,
With petals and leaves, oh so grand!
It fancied itself in a landscape of lore,
While sipping on sunlight and rain by the score.

A cat strolled by, with a curious glance,
"What's this in the pot? A leafy romance?"
The dream winked back, saying, "Join in my play!
Let's dance with the shadows, frolic all day!"

But the monster of boredom crept in with a sigh,
The dream pondered deep, "Oh, how can I fly?"
So, it danced in circles, pretending its flight,
While the cat rolled over, laughing outright!

The potted dream giggled, "Life's never so grim,
When you find joy in the smallest of whims!"
And together they laughed at the silliness found,
In the little green pot, where mirth did abound.

Melodies of Urban Greenery

In the city of cars, where the concrete does reign,
A sprout found its voice in the bustling terrain.
With roots in the pavement, it started to hum,
To the rhythm of footsteps, the city's own drum.

It twirled with the breezes, waved at the trees,
While pigeons joined in on the harmonized tease.
"Come dance with me now!" the sprout did implore,
As people looked on, giggled, and wanted to soar.

The bikes whizzed by, with the thrill of the chase,
The sprout, in response, turned its leaves into lace.
With laughter in chorus, they took to the street,
Creating a movement, lively and sweet.

And so in the city, where life passes fast,
The sprout shared its joy, making friendships that last.
In the heart of the urban, a concert took wing,
As greenery taught them the joy of a fling!

Gently Swaying in Dappled Light

In a spot where sunlight beams,
A leafy friend conspires in dreams.
With wiggles and a playful twist,
It giggles as the shadows persist.

A dance of light, a leafy shake,
A game of peek-a-boo to make.
With roots beneath, it sways with glee,
A happy jig for all to see.

The breeze plays tunes, a lively beat,
While passersby tap their feet.
A jolly green in the bright array,
This merry plant steals the day.

So here we laugh, with branches wide,
In dappled light, our joys reside.
With a gentle sway, life feels alright,
Let's dance together till the night.

Tranquility Among the Greens

In the jungle of my cozy room,
A leafy buddy shakes off gloom.
It whispers jokes in rustling leaves,
With gentle words and cheerful heaves.

A patch of green, a joyful space,
Where smiles bloom like a sunny face.
With every glance, it seems to say,
"Come join my laugh, let's play today!"

Between the pots, mischief brews,
As I forget my daily blues.
With leaf-blades sharp, it tells a tale,
Of rollicking fun without a fail.

So sip your tea and take a seat,
Among the greens where life's a treat.
We'll share a laugh, just you and I,
In this green scene, time will fly.

The Elegy of a Shrub

Oh little shrub, with stories rare,
Your leafy tales float in the air.
With every droop, you sing so sweet,
Of garden woes and insect feats.

A sad farewell, a foolish plight,
As bugs throw parties every night.
You sigh and bend, yet still you thrive,
In awkward charm, you feel alive!

Winds whisper softly through your stem,
"Cling to the laughter, don't condemn!"
In nature's jest, you find your cue,
To dance while life throws shade at you.

So here's to you, my leafy friend,
In every twist, let humor blend.
You're not alone, your roots run deep,
In laughter's garden, we'll always leap.

Chronicles of a Roommate with Roots

Meet my roommate, a leafy sage,
With roots that span across the age.
In every corner, he takes his stand,
With wise green leaves, he rules the land.

"Don't walk too close, I need my space,"
He grumbles from his leafy place.
Yet every time I spill my tea,
He giggles, claiming it's meant to be!

A mood-light maker, a growth machine,
He sprawls out wide, a verdant scene.
With tales of sunshine, rain, and cheer,
He fills my room with laughter, here!

So, raise a cup to my leafy mate,
Who keeps our stories feeling great.
In roots of humor, we will thrive,
Together in this green, we'll vibe!

The Language of Light and Leaf

In the glow of the sun, they sway with cheer,
Leaves gossiping loudly, for all to hear.
A dance of shadows, a flick of a glow,
Even the breeze can't help but show!

Bright bursts of laughter, the sunlight's jest,
With every twist and turn, they're feeling blessed.
They chat with the raindrops, sing with the breeze,
Life's a garden party—come join with ease!

Petals prance, leaves waltz, oh what a sight,
In the leafy circus, everything feels right.
Sipping sunshine, they raise their cups,
To the whims of the weather, they cheer and sup!

In this leafy language, joy takes flight,
A riddle of colors, bursting with light.
So if you pause, and lend them your ear,
You might just hear their giggles near!

Emerald Stories Unfurled

Within the green crowd, stories collide,
Whispers of mischief, giggles abide.
A sprout tales of journeys, a leaf full of glee,
Echoing laughter from each verdant spree.

With twirls and sways, they weave their lore,
A playful ballet, a leafy uproar.
Petals sneaking peeks, from their leafy embrace,
Creating a scene, a humorous space.

Bright emerald dreams dance in the air,
Plant pals exchange looks, with charming flair.
Each leaf has a secret, each stem holds a joke,
In this forest of fun, laughter's the cloak!

As sunlight spills merrily, glistening down,
Their tales intertwined, like a jester's crown.
So gather around, let the fun unwind,
In the emerald stories, joy's entwined!

Whimsical Whispers of Growth

In a playful garden, where laughter belongs,
Leaves weave their giggles, with nature's sweet songs.
Each sprout shares a tale, each stem takes a bow,
Whispering stories of 'What, when, and how?'

The sun teases blooms with a warm, gentle tickle,
While rain drops jokes, oh, how they make us giggle!
Roots in a tizzy, all tangled and tied,
They shrug with a grin, nowhere to hide!

A crooked little branch, with a comical flair,
Dresses in leaves, like it just doesn't care.
The forest alive with tales that enthrall,
Each whispering whimsy, bonding them all.

So sway with the breeze, let the chuckles unfold,
In this garden of humor, you'll find tales untold.
With a wink and a laugh, dear plants make a cheer,
In this merry green realm, there's nothing to fear!

The Succulent Journey and its Friends

On a cactus cruise, quite peculiar and spry,
Suctioned in laughter, the plants wave goodbye.
A journey through sunlight, with friends that delight,
Tales spun in spines, what a curious sight!

The succulents gather, sharing cheeky displays,
With plump little giggles, and humorous ways.
Each one a character, oh what a crew,
Riding the whims of a soft summer dew!

As they travel through gardens, a parade in green,
Showing off their charms, both funky and keen.
With a poke and a prod, they laugh at the sun,
In this joyful expedition, it's all in good fun!

So join in the frolic, embrace this wild spree,
With spines full of stories, and hearts light as glee.
On this succulent journey, each friend has a role,
In the laughter of blooms, we find our true soul!

Emotions in an Indoor Landscape

A plant sat high, looking quite grand,
It tangled with the curtain strand.
"Once a straight fellow, I swear!"
"Now a jungle, too much hair!"

Each morning it throws a leafy hiss,
"Water me, or you'll be missed!"
With every sip, it swells with glee,
As if it's downed a cup of tea.

A buzzing bee once came to flirt,
But got stuck in the foliage hurt.
"Oh dear friend, don't lose your way!"
"You'll still be here by end of day!"

Together they chuckled, what a sight,
The bee buzzed tunes with all its might.
And in this room, with laughs to check,
A plant and bee called it a trek!

The Color of Hope in a Potted World

In a pot bright green, dreams unfold,
Curled leaves like tales left untold.
"Why so lazy, dear friend?"
"You could stretch out, not just bend!"

Sunlight peeks in, it starts to dance,
"You've got the moves, give life a chance!"
With a twist and a turn, it gets bold,
Turns into stories, salvaged from old.

A sock that slipped, falls from the shelf,
"A new leaf rug, let's fancy ourselves!"
A good, good laugh as the pot proceeds,
To clutter the room with delightful weeds.

As dirt flies up, what a thrill,
Jumping plants, overtaking the sill.
Hope blooms bright, in quirky hues,
In this potted life, there's always good news!

Revelations of the Leafy Realm

In a leafy world, gossip runs wild,
"Have you seen how the dust has piled?"
In whispers of green, secrets they share,
"Does that spider plant really dare?"

Past the window, oh what a view!
"Is that a squirrel, or just a shoe?"
With every breeze, laughter does fly,
"We're better than that, oh my, oh my!"

A cat popped by, struck a bold pose,
"You won't win this round, my leafy bros!"
Leaves swayed back with a chuckle so light,
"Watch your step or you'll trip tonight!"

In the midst of chatter, they find their stride,
Each drink of sunlight, a daily ride.
For in this realm, fun never ends,
Lively green chatter, the best of friends!

The Spirit of Indoor Green

Meet the spirit, quite the fun green,
With pots and plants like you've never seen.
"I'm a powerhouse, just take a glance!"
"Who needs sun? Let's start a dance!"

Every leaf sparkles, every stem sways,
With a mischievous grin, it plays.
"Watch me grow, and bloom with pride!"
"I've got friends on the other side!"

They share tall tales of the rainy days,
"And how our roots went through a maze!"
A tiny sprout, filled with zest,
"I'll outgrow them all, just watch my jest!"

In this indoor circus, laughter bounds,
As spirits swirl in leafy sounds.
The home is bright with colors and cheer,
In a world where friendships always appear!

Urban Wilderness: A Leafy Epic

In a jungle of steel, leaves peek out,
With whispers of hope, who'd ever doubt?
They dance to the beat of a passing car,
Waving their green arms, they're sure to go far.

A stray cat meows, it's a leafy parade,
The plants roll their eyes, not easily swayed.
They giggle in sunlight, bask in delight,
Urban survivors, ready to take flight.

Pigeons look puzzled, what's growing amiss?
A basil plant's plotting a leafy kiss.
With every pot and every small tile,
They're crafting a jungle with impeccable style.

In this concrete chaos, they sing their song,
Sprouting bright dreams, so cheerful, so strong.
Who knew these greens had such wild intent?
Beneath their calm surface, a mischief is meant!

Growth Stories: Brought Indoors.

Once a sad sprout in a small little pot,
Hoping for sunshine, a whole lot of plot.
With whispered encouragement, it started to grow,
Tangled in cables, it put on a show.

Sneaking on shelves, it stretched for the light,
In shadowy corners, it gave quite a fright.
A fern gave a wink, "You're doing just fine,"
While cacti rolled eyes—"No space is confined!"

On rainy days, they throw leaf parties,
Swapping old stories, oh, how it starts!
With dust bunnies joining the leafy brigade,
Creating a ruckus, a wild masquerade!

So if you're stuck with a lonely old stem,
Remember the chaos that bursts forth from gem.
For every green leaf has a story to tell,
In laughter and joy, they know it too well!

Whispers of Green Shadows

Late at night, with the moon shining bright,
Leaves gather 'round, what a curious sight!
They exchange little secrets with soft rustling sounds,
Conspiring with shadows, giggles abound.

The pothos sips water like sipping fine wine,
While succulents boast of a shine so divine.
"Bet you can't grow an inch more than me!"
To challenge a fern—now that's pure comedy!

In corners they plot, plotting their fame,
"Let's start a band! What shall we name?"
A basil on drums, a spider plant sings,
While a peace lily strings up all the bling!

Then comes the dawn, the whispers grow soft,
As sunlight pours in, they all take off.
From shadows to sunlight, their laughter takes flight,
These leafy comedians rule the night!

The Secret Life of Leaves

Oh, the leaves that wiggle in the breeze,
Think they're so clever with fun expertise.
They slide down the windows, dodge dusty old pests,
While plotting their antics, they can't get no rest.

When humans walk by, they hold their breath,
Playing hide and seek, avoiding the mess.
A cactus winked once, "They'll never know,
The mischief we've made after the sun's glow!"

Under rugs and behind all the chairs,
They're bursting with stories, crafting new glares.
With a flip of a leaf and a flair of a vine,
They audition for roles in this grand leafy shrine!

So next time you see them, don't just glance past,
Remember, they're actors in a world that's vast.
With humor undercover, they thrive with such ease,
In the secret life where they always tease!

The Muse in the Monochrome

In a pot so round, quite debonair,
A leafy muse fills the air with flair.
Its friends often jest, 'What a sight to see!'
'Are you a plant, or a VIP?'

With blooms that dance and twirl for fun,
It claims the spotlight, never to shun.
Birds chirp in glee, a comedy show,
As vines whisper secrets, slowly they grow.

With sunlight's grace, it strikes a pose,
Who knew a plant could steal the prose?
With sunbeams tickling every green skin,
Even the shadows break out in a grin.

When folks gather round to share a tea,
The muse just winks, 'Look at me, whee!'
In this monochrome world, color takes flight,
A funny delight in the soft, sunny light.

Harmony in Flora's Embrace

In a jungle of pots, the giggles emerge,
As leaves whisper jokes, the laughter will surge.
Petals take turns in a floral charade,
While the roots twirl a dance, a root masquerade.

The mischievous vines play hide and seek,
'Find me!' they beckon, yet stay quite meek.
In the corner, a leaf laughs at the sun,
'I've got the shine, but you've got the fun!'

Every day's different in the plant party scene,
With overgrown greens, all sprightly and keen.
Indoors, they chatter, their banter's a song,
Life's a flower bed, where all jokes belong.

So join in the dance, let your worries unfurl,
With flora's embrace, it's a giggle-filled whirl.
In harmony, laughter rides on the breeze,
A jubilee blooms among the green leaves.

Lost in the Leaves' Language

Whispers of leaves, oh what a chat!
Discussing their dreams, like 'Where's my hat?'
Two plants gossip, 'Did you hear that?
The cat tried to climb, but got stuck, how 'bout that?'

In this quirky salon, the petals unfold,
As stories of sunshine and rain are retold.
The branches nod wisely, like they know it all,
Cracking up softly at the squirrel's fall.

Leaves meet in clusters, sharing their flair,
'You're looking fabulous, with that sun-kissed pair!'
Each leaf has a tale, from spring until fall,
And their humor grows stronger, never small.

So if you should wander in green's lively land,
You'll find a crowd of good jokes, oh so grand.
Lost in the leaves, in their laughter you'll dwell,
Where plants share their wisdom, and humor does swell.

Under the Canopy of Indoor Majesty

Beneath the mighty leaves, a gathering blooms,
Where laughter echoes in cozy rooms.
The ferns whisper jokes, all in good fun,
As they try to outshine the radiant sun.

'Look at my size!' boasts the grand leafy tree,
'With such great height, you can't see me!'
The smaller ones giggle, 'We're here just to tease,
You may be tall, but we dance with such ease!'

In this kingdom of green, the humor runs wild,
Each blossom a jester, each spore a sweet child.
Even the soil chuckles, tickled awake,
As roots twist and turn for a giggly shake.

So come, gather round, let the merriment flow,
Under this canopy, laughter will grow.
In the realm of the leaves, where joy finds a home,
The indoor monarchs make you feel none alone.

Whispers of Green Glory

In the corner stands a plant,
A leafy giant, oh so grand.
It sways a bit when I'm not there,
As if it knows just how to stand.

Its leaves, they whisper secrets sweet,
A chorus that cannot be beat.
I'll tease it back with playful glee,
Together, we dance to the beat.

The cats all stare as I prance near,
"Why so silly?" they seem to sneer.
But here in my garden, it's clear,
We're the stars, and we'll spread cheer.

So raise a glass to the green delight,
To my leafy friend, shining bright!
With every rustle, it makes me grin,
A pint-sized jester, no end in sight.

Elegance in Every Leaf

What a charmer, that plant I see,
With elegant leaves, it dances free.
It struts about with such finesse,
In the whims of wind, it knows no stress.

When dinner guests come to call,
It winks at them, making them all fall.
With every nod and playful sway,
It steals the scene and takes the stage.

Pictures snapped with utmost flair,
It knows it's stunning, beyond compare.
While I just chuckle, watch it show,
Who knew a plant could steal the glow?

So here's to my leafy diva,
With roots so deep, it's hard to believe-a.
Each leaf a story, each leaf a laugh,
In its grand presence, I write my path.

The Dance of Dusty Sunlight

Sunlight spills on leaves of green,
A dance floor where shadows convene.
They jiggle and jig, with a twist and turn,
As laughter grows, my heart will burn.

Dust motes swirl, in a grand ballet,
The leaves whisper, come join the fray!
"Feather your steps, be light and free,
In this moment, just be with me!"

Sipping tea while the sun shines bright,
I join my leafy friends in flight.
In that dance, we find our cheer,
With giggles echoing, loud and clear.

So let the sunlight twirl and spin,
With every wave, we let the fun begin.
For life's a dance, a vibrant song,
And in this greenery, we belong.

Secrets in the Stillness

In the stillness of the day,
Secrets beckon, come and play.
My plant just giggles, leaf by leaf,
As if in jest, it hides belief.

Dust gathers, but who would know?
In its world, time seems to slow.
With every pause, a laugh does bloom,
In the green, I find my room.

Quiet chuckles shared in space,
Between us grows a cozy place.
For in its silence, mischief grows,
A friendship deep that only glows.

So here in corners, in golden light,
We hold our secrets, pure delight.
With every whisper, we're not alone,
In this still world, we call our own.

Echoes of Nature's Solitude

In a pot where sunlight beams,
A leafy champion quietly dreams.
Waving arms in dance so spry,
Whispering secrets to the shy.

With a soil so rich and deep,
This green fellow skips sleep.
Roots that wiggle, leaves that sway,
Making magic, come what may.

Encounters with dust bunnies galore,
Every corner hides more folklore.
He chuckles at the curious flies,
Witty jests amid nature's sighs.

Branches jive, snapping to the beat,
A quirky symphony, oh so sweet.
In this space, joy takes a ride,
Nature's laughter spread far and wide.

Leaves of Memory Unfold

One leaf said to another with glee,
'Got any wild plans? Come sit with me!'
Together they plotted a grand escape,
To travel beyond their pot's landscape.

Sneaking out when the humans nap,
Creating mischief, a leafy trap.
Swapping tales from the window sill,
Drawing giggles with a daring thrill.

They devised a game of hide and seek,
With dust bunnies playing hideaway chic.
Bouncing light, their laughter swirled,
In a green kingdom, they twirled and twirled.

Oh, the stories they spun, so quite absurd,
Of time-traveling roots and flying birds.
Just two leaves in a pot so vast,
Crafting memories that forever last.

The Quiet Transformations of Nature

In the still of the early morn,
A dancer piques from silence, reborn.
Leaves unfurl with a playful quake,
Nature's jest, a lively awake.

With every wrinkle and gentle fold,
A story of change, humorously told.
Who's the comedian? The sun, perhaps,
As shadows waltz, the plant now claps.

Fiddlin' with light, a green façade,
With mischief brewing, a sly charade.
Roots giggle softly beneath the earth,
A comedy show since their birth.

As seasons shift and laughter grows,
The vine climbs up, but no one knows.
In this pot of giggles and cheer,
Nature whispers, 'Come draw near!'

Portrait of a Room's Green Guardian

A leafy guardian stands so brave,
With roots that dance like they misbehave.
In every breath, a chuckle's shared,
As sunlight filters, none are scared.

He surveys the room with a clever glance,
Watching humans stumble in their dance.
'Careful, dear friends, don't trip on my leaves!
Nature's humor, oh how it weaves!'

Amongst the furniture and scattered toys,
This verdant soul finds endless joys.
In laughter, he sways, the jokes in the air,
A guardian of giggles, beyond compare.

In his verdant crown, the good times thrive,
A jester in green, keeping dreams alive.
Through sunlight's curtain, glimmers of cheer,
To all who wander, his spirit draws near.

Nature's Gallery on Display

In a pot so snug, a plant does sway,
Leaves are dancing, come what may.
Critters peek in, their eyes so wide,
Wondering who calls this home inside.

One day it twitched, a leaf gave a laugh,
A curious squirrel stopped for a gaff.
"Is this a tree?" he chuckled in jest,
"Or just an oversized broccoli quest?"

Each dawn it stretches, reaching for light,
A yoga pose, oh what a sight!
Scaring the cat with its leafy flares,
A green little menace, none can compare.

With friends all around, the pot feels so grand,
In this tiny world, the weirdest of bands.
Nature's gallery, a grand display,
All we need's a laugh to brighten the day.

Whims of a Potted Universe

In a quirky pot, a cosmos does spin,
A plant from Pluto, who wants to fit in.
"Earthling!" it shouts with a leafy delight,
"I bring the galactic dance to your night!"

A snail with shades claims to be the star,
While worms cheer him on from their earthen bar.
The soil giggles, a ticklish mound,
Whispers of mischief are always around.

A spider declares, "I've spun tales thrice!"
"My webs tell of worlds that are oh-so-nice!"
The lily blinks twice, its petals in glee,
"Join in the fun, you've gotta be free!"

With each little breeze, the plant takes a spin,
In this pot of wonders, let the laughter begin.
An ordinary plant, but with magic tucked in,
Whims of the universe, let the journey commence!

The Art of Nurtured Dreams

In a bright little corner, dreams start to sprout,
A green masterpiece, there's no doubt.
With each drop of water, it leans with a grin,
Whispering secrets of where it's been.

A sprinkle of sun and a dash of good cheer,
It frames the day's canvas, so vivid and clear.
Colorful thoughts float about in the air,
As leaves reach for the sky without any care.

Each night it plots, plotting the stars,
While sleeping orchids dream of little cars.
A painted imagination, it sways to the tune,
The art of nurturing under the moon.

With pots full of joy and smiles to bestow,
This garden's a gallery, putting on a show.
No ribbon for best in this verdant scheme,
Just laughter and love, and the beauty of dream!

Melodies of Domestic Flora

In the heart of the home, a symphony starts,
Leaves play the notes, oh how they impart!
Each rustle and sway, a lively refrain,
Nature's own chorus, sweet music in grain.

The cacti chime in, their prickles so brave,
While daisies do waltzes, in a rhythmic wave.
The pot's got its groove, it's the place to be,
With each petal's dance, wild and free!

A fern taps its feet, with a flourish and flair,
While the ivy shows off with a twist of its hair.
A cheerful duet, in pots side by side,
Melodies ringing, come join for the ride!

So gather around, let the laughter revive,
With domestic flora, we'll truly thrive.
In this silly jig, the fun never ends,
For nature's a party, where everyone blends!

Reflections of Earthbound Bliss

In a pot so round and brown,
A leafy crown, my quirky clown.
Does it know it's living high?
On my shelf, it waves goodbye!

Sipping sunlight, oh so sweet,
Those little roots dance on their feet.
Yet here I am, just watching close,
Wishing I could be like those!

Watering with routines so grand,
Chatting with my green friend so planned.
It sways and nods, a cheeky tease,
I laugh, it laughs; we're both at ease.

Green and growing, what a joke,
Am I the plant or just its bloke?
So, here I stay, in leafy bliss,
Living life like this, how could I miss?

The Guardian of Soil and Sun

Sitting proud on table's edge,
Guardian of plant and hedge.
Basking in the warm sunlight,
A leafy warrior, what a sight!

With every droplet, cheers arise,
As if it sings under blue skies.
Oh what fun, my earthy friend,
Together we shall blend and bend!

A sentinel of pot and earth,
Who knew it had such lively mirth?
Each sprout demands a giddy dance,
While I simply take a chance.

I chuckle at the roots below,
Stealing whispers, secrets flow.
What are we, a pair of fools?
Flora, friend, breaking all the rules!

Whispers from the Indoor Eden

In the corner, green and bright,
Swaying gently, pure delight.
Whispers echo through the air,
What's that? A leaf's secret flair?

Chattering leaves in breezy cheer,
Each rustle brings stories near.
Oh, how I wish they'd divulge,
What the houseplants feel and indulge!

It tickles me to see them thrive,
Little green folks come alive.
Funny how they steal the show,
While I sit and soak, ho-ho!

So here we jest, the indoor gang,
Leaves a-dancing, hearts a-clang!
In this Eden—planty and true,
Growing giggles, me and you.

Tales of Growth and Resilience

Up they reach, those leafy dreams,
Daring sunlight's warm regimes.
Poking fun at every turn,
For more of life, they boldly yearn!

Each twist and curl, a story spun,
Who knew that plants could be so fun?
With every sprout, a tiny jest,
A show of growth that beats the rest!

They poke their heads past every edge,
In lovely greens, they make their pledge.
To thrive, to joy, to dance in glee,
As if the world's a grand glee.

So lift your glass to roots below,
To every leaf, let laughter flow!
With quirky quirks, they entertain,
These greens bring joy, we share the gain!

Silhouettes of Nature's Song

In the corner, green and spry,
A leaf once waved, oh my oh my.
It swayed to tunes of playful breeze,
And danced with glee among the trees.

Its neighbors whispered tales so bright,
Of sunlight joys by day and night.
A pot of jokes from soil it fed,
With roots that chuckled, dreams in bed.

I caught it snickering at the sun,
"You're getting bold, don't be outdone!"
With every glare, it puffed out wide,
A leafy grin it could not hide.

So here we are, this leafy crew,
With laughter sprouting, just like dew.
In this green realm, joy never ends,
With every whim, nature transcends.

Canvas of Green Resilience

A jungle in a tiny pot,
Each leaf a hero, bold and hot.
With every stretch and every sigh,
It claims its turf, oh my oh my!

Abandon the scissors, let's have a spree,
Why trim a plant that loves to be free?
It mocks the snips with leafy pride,
Hiding secrets it will not bide.

With popcorn roots and breezy laughs,
It sketches life with leafy drafts.
Neighbors poke fun as we stroll by,
This lively plant cannot be shy.

In sun and storm, it thrives with flair,
A comical dance, no need for care.
So let's toast to greens, quite irreverent,
In nature's world, they're the real resident.

An Ode to a Leafy Companion

Oh leafy friend, in pot you dwell,
With tales of growth you're sure to tell.
Each tendril twirls in chaos' light,
A whirl of green, your heart so bright.

You tickle dust and sip the air,
In every breeze, your woes laid bare.
And when I trip, you seem to giggle,
My wooden floor, your favorite riddle.

Such vibrant jests you spin each day,
As sunlight streams in golden play.
You wear the season's clothes with pride,
A leafy jest that won't subside.

So here's a cheer to your zestful show,
In corners where warm, bright moments grow.
For every giggle, every dance,
With you, dear leaf, I've found my chance.

Soliloquy of the Indoor Universe

In a realm where sunlight spills,
Among the drapes, reality thrills.
A leafy squad in a dance-off bold,
Whispers of green, stories told.

The dust bunnies watch as we do our thing,
A concert of laughter, oh how we sing!
With pots as our stage, in wild delight,
We sway to the music of the night.

Each leaf has a tune, a silly rhyme,
Collective chuckles that age like wine.
A banter of photosynthesis so spry,
Who knew plants could quip and sigh?

With each sip of water, our giggles grow,
In this indoor haven, our laughter flows.
So here's to the greens, quite absurd,
In the universe of pots, we joyfully heard.

The Heartbeat of Houseplants

In a pot, quite snug and round,
A leafy lad makes funny sounds.
He wiggles, jiggles, boogies too,
Dancing 'round with the morning dew.

His friends all cheer, the cacti clap,
While the fern provides a leafy map.
"Oh, come and join!" the ivy calls,
But everyone's rooted, stuck in their stalls.

The little guy has quite the show,
Wobbling where the sunlight glows.
"Give me a sip!" he cries in glee,
"Or this party's just not for me!"

And as he sways, they burst with laughter,
Blades and brambles in silly banter.
Each rustle brings a giggling cheer,
In the world of plants, there's joy, my dear!

Enchantment in a Corner Pot

In the corner, a shy plant hides,
Wishing for friends, though it confides.
With leaves that curl and twirl in glee,
It plots a scheme to be wild and free.

A gnome nearby starts to grin wide,
With a twinkle that can't be denied.
"Let's throw a party!" he shouts with pride,
The corners of rooms dance side by side.

Balloons of petals, a feast of light,
Each leaf sharing stories, pure delight.
"Let's dance till dusk, and sing till dawn!
But don't trip on roots, come on, come on!"

The mystery plant at last joins in,
A giggle erupts, a leafy spin.
Together they revel, bright and spry,
In their pot, beneath the vast sky.

Harmony Among Stalks

A quirky bunch, they stand so tall,
Each stalk a character, short or small.
With chatter and cheer, they gather near,
Swapping funny tales, laughter clear.

The basil brags of fragrant grace,
While mint jokes about a toothy space.
"Oh, look at you!" the thyme does tease,
"Your scent's so strong, it brings bees to their knees!"

The violet spins a colorful tale,
Of a trip that went off the rails.
"I sneezed once, and oh, what a sight,
A gardener fell, it gave quite a fright!"

As shadows lengthen and night draws near,
The stalks still giggle, spreading cheer.
With roots entwined, they give a shout,
In harmony, no room for doubt!

A Fable of Verdant Serenity

In the garden, all things green,
A fable unfolds, quite serene.
With whispers of joy in the gentle breeze,
They share their secrets, if you please.

A leaf once snorted, just for fun,
It rolled on the soil, under the sun.
"Watch out!" cried thyme, giggling wide,
"Or the compost may just be your ride!"

With each little chuckle, roots twist and twine,
Creating a symphony, leafy and fine.
"Let's be merry!" said the old oak grand,
"As we dance together, hand in hand."

So in this garden of fronds and cheer,
The tales of joy, we hold so dear.
Where silliness grows, like weeds in bloom,
In verdant serenity, dispelling gloom!

Beneath the Surface of Nurtured Soil

In the dark where roots do play,
Wiggles and giggles all day.
Whispers of worms, a crazy crew,
Dancing around in muddy stew.

They tell silly jokes, and they laugh,
Roots tickle each other, a leaf's gaff.
Nestled in dirt, they twirl and twist,
Who knew that compost could hold such a tryst?

Under the charades, they plot a scheme,
A leaf team up for a bright sunbeam.
They challenge the bugs for the best of the sun,
With giggles and wiggles, they're having such fun!

Rhapsody of Petiole and Blade

The blades compose, a leafy tune,
Strumming sunlight, a sunlit rune.
Petiole conducts, with flair so bright,
A waltz with the wind, such a funny sight!

Chopped up in laughter, in breezy air,
Swinging and swaying without a care.
Petiole spins, whispers a joke,
Leaves burst with laughter, as the sunlight awoke.

Each rustle a riff, a trumpet's blast,
Fiddles with laughter, oh how they last!
Nature's own band, a riot in green,
Making music with joy, quite the scene!

A Leaf's Dream in a Concrete World

Up in the sky, a leaf takes a nap,
Dreaming of sunshine, in nature's lap.
Here in the cracks, where the lost dreams grow,
Slapstick adventures in the city's flow.

Hitching a ride on a passing breeze,
Dodging the pigeons, and big busy bees.
Plant socks and frolic wherever they may,
In a world of gray, they find the ballet.

Shimmer and sparkle, on rooftops so high,
Waving to clouds while hot dogs fly by.
With tangled humor, they twirl and sway,
Bringing a grin to the dull city's day!

The Heartbeat of Urban Flora

In the cracks of asphalt, where green things peek,
Little plants giggle, while humans sneak.
Chirping with life, a rhythmic beat,
Grass blades dance to the pulse of the street.

Ferns whisper secrets while tumbling along,
Joining the laughter, a botanical song.
Petals in twirls, a whimsical show,
In the heart of the city, they put on a flow!

Vines with a mind, they climb and entwine,
Sipping on sunshine, on city's fine wine.
Roots stretch and chuckle, as sidewalks parade,
Creating a symphony, urban charade!

The Legacy of Branch and Leaf

In a garden full of green,
Stands a plant quite serene.
With leaves like giant fans,
It dances to unseen plans.

The neighbors watch in awe,
As it bends without a flaw.
One day it tried to wave,
And knocked over a brave knave!

Its legacy is quite absurd,
A tale no one has heard.
Chasing cats up the street,
With roots made of quick feet!

Yet in the moon's soft light,
It becomes quite the sight.
Branching tales of strange glee,
In a whimsical spree!

Serenity in Leafy Corners

In corners where shadows play,
A leafy dance leads the way.
Whispers tickle the air,
As branches spin in flair.

Crazy leaves try to chat,
While squirrels nod and pat.
"What's the secret?" they plead,
The plant just smirks, "You'll see!"

Laughter echoes soft and low,
As the gardens put on a show.
With roots that wiggle and twirl,
It's the quirkiest plant in the world!

So join the leafy parade,
In the foliage, don't be afraid.
For in every leafy nook,
There's a punchline to the book!

Breath of the Verdant Heart

The heart of the green beats loud,
In a jungle of leaves, oh so proud.
It tickles the air with glee,
Blowing thoughts like a leaf on a spree.

Caterpillars drop by for tea,
And ask, "What's the recipe?"
"Just add a sprinkle of joy,"
The plant giggles like a schoolboy!

Each petal whispers around,
Where silliness can be found.
With a puff and a sway,
It brings chuckles into the fray!

So breathe deep this verdant joke,
Let laughter break like a cloak.
For in each gentle sigh,
Life's comedy learns to fly!

Petals in a Dusty Window

In a window with dust so thick,
Petals plot their little trick.
They flutter and flap with glee,
Waiting for someone to see.

With a wink and a nudge,
They squeal, "Let's not judge!"
For what's inside may surprise,
A humor that brightly flies.

Visitors peek with a grin,
As petals begin to spin.
They tickle your nose just right,
Causing sneezes of sheer delight!

So clean the glass, let it shine,
Glimpse the antics, oh divine!
In every dusty corner found,
Laughter blooms all around!

Rebirth Among Houseplants

In a pot sat a plant with a grin,
Its leaves doing a twisty spin.
It danced through the light, oh what a sight,
Claiming the room is its fun little inn.

A spider plant smiled, then jumped from the shelf,
Said, 'Life's too short not to have a good yelp!'
The cacti all chuckled, 'We're stuck like glue!'
'Come join the ruckus, forget all your health!'

The snake plant whispered, 'I've stories with flair,
About lizards who climb up my leaves with great care.'
They giggled together, what a feel-good,
In the bright, green kingdom, they thrived everywhere.

So next time you water, don't just see green,
These leafy pals know more than they seem,
They're plotting and giggling, oh what a dream,
Their fun little world is the best kind of team.

Musings of a Nature Companion

Oh, the ivy complained, 'I'm tangled and shy,
With one leaf in the air and one eye on a fly.'
'Those clouds overhead seem a bit too gray,
Can someone explain why I can't just sway?'

The fern chuckled warmly, 'You're always so keen!
Don't worry, dear ivy; it's just a bad scene.
When sunlight peeks through, we'll all shimmy and shake,

But for now, dear friend, let's make room for a bean!'

A pothos chimed in, 'With stories to share,
Of snails and their journeys, let's roll out a chair.'
They sang their own ballad, a chorus so bright,
Plant gossip and laughter filled up the fresh air.

So plants sit together, with humor in tow,
Spinning wild yarns that only they know.
While we humans prattle about work and the grind,
These green little friends bask in joy's sweet flow.

Unraveled Stories in Pot and Soil

Deep in a pot, sat an elder sage,
Whose roots told tales beyond any age.
With a wink and a nod, he'd chuckle and tease,
'What's your secret, old friend? Give us a page!'

'The secret,' he smirked, 'is to dance like the breeze,
To wiggle your leaves with the greatest of ease.'
His comrades all rocked, like they heard a fine song,
'For plants without laughter just become a tease!'

The flower beside him chimed in with glee,
'Sometimes I wonder who's as bright as me?'
They laughed 'til they shivered, a joyful cocoon,
In this greenery haven, the world felt so free.

So pot after pot, they wove fun-filled lore,
At times they'd forget what they'd been grown for.
Instead, they just bloomed with warmth in their hearts,
Growing bonds and laughs forevermore.

Symphony of the Indoor Jungle

In my room, there's a leafy king,
He shakes his leaves, does a little swing.
Ferns nod their heads, quite the scene,
As our playful plants dance like a dream.

A spider plays drums, with a tiny tune,
While the sun spills light like a cheerful balloon.
Each leaf a story, a quirky tale,
In my jungle home, we set our sail.

The cat creeps close, oh what a sight,
A pounce on a vine, what a delight!
Laughter bursts forth, echoes around,
This verdant place is joy unbound.

So join the fun, bring your own cheer,
In this wild, green world, there's nothing to fear.
With every twist of leaf and vine,
We'll write our ode, our life divine.

Shadows Beneath the Canopy

Beneath the green, the shadows play,
They twirl and leap, in a merry way.
A pot with dirt whispers to the floor,
Mossy secrets that we adore.

There's a gnome tucked behind a fern,
With a mischievous grin, it's his turn.
He twirls his beard, with delight anew,
As plants giggle, all in a queue.

The dog thinks it's a game of chase,
Through twisting vines, in this wild place.
But each step's a dance, full of jest,
Our jungle's a stage—come be our guest!

So sit awhile and join the fun,
In shadows where laughter has just begun.
The greenery waits, invites with glee,
In our kooky jungle, just you and me.

Lyrical Roots and Soaring Dreams

Roots are busy, wiggling wide,
In their underworld, they take pride.
They whisper tunes to the leaves above,
An orchestra of life, a symphony of love.

A squirrel leaps in, with a daring flair,
Stealing a nut from a clumsy pair.
The pot-tending plants peek and giggle,
As the furry thief takes a wily wiggle.

A sunbeam dances, oh what a sight,
Playing tag with shadows, day or night.
And in this laughter, dreams take flight,
With each rustle and chuckle, all feels right.

So gather 'round, let your worries cease,
In this light-hearted space, find peace.
With roots and leaves, and critters galore,
We'll sing our song forevermore.

Vibrance of a Living Space

In my cozy nook, plants come alive,
With viney laughter, they surely thrive.
Pothos swinging, the peace lily grins,
As the orange cat pretends he spins.

The jade sings jokes in whispers clear,
To the cactus provoked, "I'll poke you, dear!"
Bright colors clash in a joyful spree,
In this ecosystem, we all agree.

Guests come over, and the fun begins,
Greenery fluffs up, boasting its fins.
Together we laugh, play hide and seek,
In our living space, we're all unique.

So here's a toast to the plants we share,
A garden of joy, a lively affair.
In this vibrant haven, the humor flows,
With every leaf, our happiness grows.

A Palette of Homegrown Dreams

In the corner, a leafy dream,
Dancing stalks sway with gleam.
Pots whisper tales of the sun,
Where roots gather to have some fun.

With watering can, I take my aim,
A wild plant party, oh what a game!
Soil splatters on my new shoes bright,
As I giggle through the soil fight.

Every leaf, a cheeky grin,
Nature's art, forever in.
Though one plant droops with a frown,
I swear it wears a leafy crown!

In this vivid garden hue,
Laughter grows like morning dew.
Sprouts of joy in every seam,
Homegrown smirks, a leafy dream.

Interludes in the Indoor Garden

Amidst the pots, a ruckus plays,
Tiny critters join the fray.
With a sprout that teases the sun,
It prances around, what fun!

Fingers dance in the dirt so deep,
Monsters under roots don't sleep.
A leafy wizard in disguise,
Casting spells with leafy sighs.

Every twist, a strange ballet,
Surreal views on display.
The green conspirators plot their tricks,
With roots, they weave their leafy mix.

Petals chuckle in the breeze,
Whispers float through trees with ease.
This indoor stage, a vivid play,
With nature's humor on full display.

The Symphony of Petiole and Pulse

In this house where green prevails,
Music sprouts and never fails.
Leaves clap hands, and roots all sing,
As pots gather for a swing.

A velvet leaf like a ceaseless drum,
Plays a tune that makes me hum.
Fronds sway like a charming dancer,
While culprits munch, what a romancer!

In a crescendo of green delight,
Nonsensical laughter fills the night.
Leaves giggle in their leafy frames,
Plotting to steal all the fame.

So let's cheer this planty show,
As the indoor breezes blow.
With every pulse, a fiesta grows,
A symphony where laughter flows.

Life Wrapped in Green Tapestry

Thread by thread, nature weaves,
A tapestry of funny leaves.
Dancing light through windows bright,
Tickles plants till they feel light.

In cozy corners, mischief blooms,
With plants that dance in their rooms.
The shades of green wear silly hats,
Swapping stories with fluffy cats.

A quirky vine climbs the wall,
Feigning elegance, but prone to fall.
Sprouts of laughter echo here,
Life unfolds with cheer and cheer.

As green wraps tight around my soul,
In every snicker, a heart feels whole.
Through giggles of leaves, love will glide,
A cheerful life wears nature's pride.

www.ingramcontent.com/pod-product-compliance
Lightning Source LLC
Chambersburg PA
CBHW070312120526
44590CB00017B/2645